12 Quizzes on

Classical Composers

BY GAIL MCGAFFIGAN

Based on works of Thomas Tapper which are now in the public domain

Discover other titles by Gail McGaffigan at
http://www.amazon.com/-/e/B008P54VVQ

Table of Contents

Quizzes

Answers

-

Bach

1. In what year did Bach die?
2. Name an American who was alive at the same time.
3. What famous castle can be seen from the streets of Eisenach?
4. What other great German composer lived in Bach's time?
5. What instruments could Bach play?
6. For what purpose did Bach travel from place to place, as a boy?
7. What was the name of Sebastian's father?
8. Who was Hans, the Player?
9. How many children had Bach? Which two were musicians?
10. Name three pieces by Bach that you have heard.

<u>Beethoven</u>

1. When and where was Beethoven born?
2. Who was his first teacher?
3. What did his father do?
4. How old was Ludwig when he left school?
5. What description of him as a boy in school has been given?
6. How old was he when he first played in public?
7. What composition of his was first to be published? How old was he at the time?
8. Which of his teachers took great interest in him?
9. What did he say about the little boy's future?
10. Where did Beethoven go when he was sixteen years old, and why?
11. With what two great masters did he study?
12. What composer, as a little boy, went to see Beethoven?
13. How did he describe him?
14. Name some of the forms of music which Beethoven composed.
15. Write a list of music by Beethoven that you have heard.
16. What is a concerto? a sonata?
17. How old was Beethoven when he died?

<u>Chopin</u>

1. In what country was Chopin born?

2. In what two great cities did he live?

3. In what year was Chopin born?

4. What other composer was born about the same time?

5. How old was Chopin when he first appeared in public?

6. What two works had he already composed when he set out for Paris?

7. Who were some of the people who welcomed Chopin to Paris?

8. Name some of the great cities in which he played.

9. What led Chopin to want to leave Paris?

10. Why did he change his mind and remain there?

11. What great German composer discovered Chopin to be a genius?

12. Name some great writers and composers who kept at work even though

they were not in the best of health.

13. In what country was Grieg born?

14. In what city was Mozart born?

15. In what two countries did Handel live?

16. What famous river flows by the City of Warsaw?

17. Name some of the kinds of music that Chopin composed.

18. What music by Chopin have you heard?

Grieg

1. When and where was Grieg born?
2. Name some famous men of his country.
3. Who was his first teacher?
4. Through whose advice did he go to the Conservatory at Leipzig?
5. What Danish composer gave Grieg good advice about his compositions?
6. Who were some of Grieg's teachers?
7. What composition by Grieg was given first prize in the contest in
Sweden?
8. What famous song did Grieg dedicate to Mina Hagerup?
9. Tell about Grieg's visit to Liszt in Rome.
10. Name as many of his compositions as you can. How many have you
heard?
11. Tell what you know about Grieg's personal appearance.
12. When did Grieg die? How old was he?
13. Who was Jenny Lind?

Handel

1. In what year was Handel born?
2. What other great composer was born the same year in Germany?
3. What was the profession of Handel's father?
4. How did it come about that Handel was allowed to study music?
5. Who was Handel's first teacher?
6. What subjects did he study with his teacher?
7. What instruments did Handel play?
8. In what other cities and countries did Handel live?
9. Of what country did he become a citizen?
10. Name some of the famous composers of the day whom Handel knew.
11. What kinds of music did Handel write?
12. What form of music is the _Messiah_?
13. What was the "Water Music?"
14. How did Handel come to write it?
15. When did Handel die and where was he buried?

Haydn

1. Where and in what year was Joseph Haydn born?
2. By what name was he known at home?
3. Who was his first teacher?
4. What studies had he at St. Stephen's?
5. With what distinguished family did he live for many years?
6. Give the names of some of the distinguished composers whom he knew.
7. What great composer was his pupil for a time in Vienna?
8. Why did Mozart think that Haydn should not travel through so many
strange countries?
9. What two great works did he write after he returned from England?
10. In what year did Haydn die?
11. In what year did George Washington die?

Liszt

1. When and where was Franz Liszt born?
2. Who was his first teacher?
3. What was his father's occupation? With what family did he live?
4. Where was his mother born?
5. With whom did Franz study piano in Vienna?
6. What famous musician did he meet in Vienna?
7. Name two people whom he met in Paris.
8. What great composer of opera did he assist?
9. Name some operas that Liszt produced at Weimar.
10. In what Italian city did Liszt live?
11. Whose songs did he arrange for piano?
12. What great musician's life was written by Franz Liszt?
13. When and where did Franz Liszt die?

Mozart

1. In what country was Mozart born?
2. In what city was Mozart born?
3. Where did Mozart play before the Emperor and the Empress?
4. Did Mozart play games and have a good time like other boys?
5. Why did people ask Mozart to play upon the harpsichord with a cloth
stretched over the keys?
6. Whose compositions did the King of England ask Mozart to play?
7. What great American patriot was born in the same year as Haydn?
8. Which lived the longer life, Haydn or Mozart?
9. Name three pieces you have heard by Mozart.
10. Was Mozart spoiled by meeting many people?

<u>Schubert</u>

1. Where was Schubert born?
2. When was Schubert born?
3. Name two American authors who were boys when Schubert was born.
4. Name two composers who lived at the same time.
5. What was the father of Franz Schubert?
6. Who taught Schubert harmony?
7. Give the name of a famous song by Schubert.
8. What famous musician died in Vienna when Schubert was twelve years old?
9. Who was the noted singer who helped to make Schubert's songs famous?
10. When did Schubert die?

<u>Schumann</u>

1. In what country was Schumann born?
2. Can you name some pieces for the piano composed by Schumann?
3. What did he write when he was a little boy?
4. What great pianist did Robert hear when a boy?
5. Name some famous Americans who were boys when Robert was going to
school.
6. Who wrote Hiawatha? Tanglewood Tales?
7. With whom did Robert Schumann study the piano?
8. Whom did Robert Schumann marry?
9. Tell what you know about her.
10. Where did Schumann teach?
11. Mention some of his friends.
12. What does the composer picture for us in the "Happy Farmer?"
13. Which composer friend did Schumann honor with a piece spelling the man's name in notes
14. In what year was Schumann born?
15. For what type of compositions is Schumann best known?
16. How did he help people find new composers?
17. What two great misfortunes came to Schumann during his life?

<u>Verdi</u>

1. When and where was Verdi born?
2. How old was he when he died?
3. Can you mention three works of Verdi that are not operas?
4. How many operas can you name from memory?
5. What instruments did Verdi play as a boy?
6. When was Verdi's first opera performed?
7. What two great operas did Verdi compose following a 16-year break?
8. What did Verdi love to do besides compose music?
9. What is a Spinet?
10. In what famous city did he study as a boy?
11. How many operas, in all, did Verdi compose?
12. What country is the setting for "Aida?"
13. To what did Verdi devote his fortune?

<u>Wagner</u>

1. What form of music did Richard Wagner compose?

2. When was he born?

3. Can you name some of the musicians who lived when Richard Wagner was
a boy?

4. How many characters from the Dickens' novel can you name from memory?

5. In what opera by Richard Wagner is "The Prize Song?"

6. Who sings it?

7. Tell what kind of a man Beckmesser is.

8. Who was the jolly cobbler singer?

9. What happened to Beckmesser in the contest with Walter?

10. What sort of characters occur in Wagner's operas?

11. See if you can describe each of these: Donner, Fafner, Mime, Freia,
Wotan.

12. What is the name of the house in which Richard Wagner was born?

13. Tell some of the things he did when he was a boy.

14. Who composed Oberon?

15. What other opera did this composer write?

16. What should we remember about childhood thoughts?

Answers

Answers: Bach

1. 1750
2. Benjamin Franklin
3. Wartburg
4. Handel
5. Clavier/clavichord and organ
6. To hear fine organists
7. Johannesburg Ambrosius Bach
8. An ancestor of J.S. Bach,Hans was the violinist son of Veit Bach, a miller who sang while he worked.
9. 20; Friedmann and Philipp Emanuel.
10. Answers will vary

Answers: Beethoven

1. December 16, 1770, Bonn, Germany
2. His father
3. He was a singer at the Chapel of the Elector.
4. 13
5. Shy and quiet, he talked little and took no interest in games.
6. 8
7. "Variations on Dressler's March;" 10
8. Neefe
9. "If he goes on as he has begun, he will some day be a second Mozart."
10. To Vienna to see Mozart
11. Mozart and Haydn
12. Carl Czerny

13. "Beethoven was dressed in a dark gray jacket and trousers of some
long-haired material, which reminded me of the description of Robinson
Crusoe I had just been reading. The jet-black hair stood upright on his
head. A beard, unshaven for several days, made still darker his
naturally swarthy face. I noticed also, with a child's quick perception,
that he had cotton wool which seemed to have been dipped in some yellow
fluid in both ears. His hands were covered with hair, and the fingers
were very broad, especially at the tips."

14. Symphonies, concertos, sonatas, songs, choral and chamber music.

15. Answers will vary.

16. concerto: a piece of music, usually with 3 or more movements, composed for a solo instrument accompanied by a group of instruments, typically an orchestra; sonata: a piece of music, usually with 3 or more movements, composed for a solo instrument, usually accompanied by a keyboard instrument.

17. 57

Answers: Chopin
1. Poland
2. Warsaw and Paris
3. 1809
4. Mendelssohn
5. 9
6. two piano concertos for the piano

7. Liszt, Berlioz, Meyerbeer, Heine, and Berlioz

8. Vienna, Berlin, and Munich

9. Only a few people were present at his first concert and for quite a while he had no pupils.

10. His friend, Franz Liszt, convinced him to play at the home of Baron Rothschild, where he was so successful, many present begged to study with him.

11. Schumann

12. Milton, Beethoven, Stevenson, and Grieg

13. Norway

14. Salzburg

15. Germany and England

16. Vistula

17. nocturne, waltz, mazurka, impromptu, concerto, polonaise, etude

18. Answers will vary.

Answers: Grieg

1. June 15, 1843, near Bergen, Norway

2. Gade, Nordraak, Ibsen, Bjornson, and Svendsen

3. His mother

4. Ole Bull, the violinist

5. Niels Gade

6. Richter

7. "Autumn"

8. "I Love Thee"

9. He met with Liszt, who asked Grieg to play. Then, Liszt took Grieg's manuscript and played it at sight, and was delighted. When Grieg bade good-bye to Liszt, the famous pianist said to him "Keep on, you have talent and ability. Do not let any one discourage or frighten you."

10. Answers will vary

11. In appearance Grieg was short and rather bent in figure. His hands were
thin, but fine and strong for the piano, although one of them had been
crushed in an accident. His eyes were deep blue. They looked straight at
you and were full of life and kindness.

12. September 3, 1907 at the age of 64.

13. Jenny Lind, known as "the Swedish nightingale," was loved
not only for her wonderful voice but for her kindness and noble nature.

Answers: Handel

1. 1685
2. Johann Sebastian Bach
3. surgeon/barber
4. When Handel was seven years old, his father went by coach to visit someone, who was in the service of the Duke of
Saxe-Weissenfels. Handel begged his father to let him come, too. His father said he was too young to go so far. However, the boy followed on foot. Finally the father ordered the coach to stop and take him in, and they continued on to the castle. One day the Duke himself heard him play. He was astonished at the young boy's skill. Calling the father into his presence, he pointed out how wrong it was to deny the boy the right to study music. "The world," he said, "should have the good of your son's great ability."
5. Zachau
6. harmony, counterpoint, canon, and fugue
7. organ, hautbois (oboe), violin, and harpsichord

8. Berlin, Hamburg, Italy, London, Hanover

9. England

10. Johann Mattheson, Corelli, Alessandro Scarlatti, Domenico Scarlatti

11. Fugues, suites, some operas, oratorios, works for organ, piano, and chamber orchestra.

12. Oratorio

13. A set of 25 pieces to be played from a boat during the coronation of George I, King of England.

14. After accepting the post of Capellmeister from the Elector of Hanover, Handel went visited England, and, liking it, decided to stay. While he was there, the Elector of Hanover became George I, King of England. Handel was afraid the king would bear a grudge against him for not returning to his post. A friend arranged for Handel to compose some music for the king's coronation. When Handel presented "Water Music," the king liked it so much, he invited Handel to join him on the royal boat.

15. Good Friday, 1759; Westminster Abbey

Answers: Haydn

1. Austria, 1732.

2. Sepperl

3. a schoolmaster town of Hainburg, named Frankh

4. music studies in singing, violin, and piano, and school studies in Religion, Latin, Writing, and Arithmetic.

5. The Esterhazys

6. Metastasio, Porpora, Gluck, Beethoven, Wolfgang Mozart and his father, Leopold Mozart

7. Beethoven

8. Mozart said he was too old, and did not know foreign languages well enough to travel through many countries.

9. "The Creation"and "The Seasons"

10. 1809

11. 1799

Answers: Liszt

1. October 22, 1811, in Raiding, Hungary.

2. His father

3. His father was the Esterhazys property steward, so the Liszt family lived with them.

4. Austria

5. Carl Czerny

6. Beethoven

7. Chopin, Victor Hugo

8. Richard Wagner

9. "Lohengrin," "Tannhauser," and "The Flying Dutchman" by
Richard Wagner; "Genoveva" and "Manfred" by Robert Schumann;
"Alfonzo and Estrella" by Franz Schubert.

10. Rome

11. Franz Schubert

12. Frederic Chopin

13. 1886, Rome

Answers: Mozart

1. Austria

2. Salzburg

3. Vienna

4. Yes.

5. To see how he could play without seeing the keys
6. Handel and Bach
7. George Washington
8. Haydn
9. Answers will vary
10. No.

Answers: Schubert

1. Vienna
2. January 31, 1797
3. Washington Irving, James Fenimore Cooper, and William Cullen Bryant
4. Czerny, Von Weber, Rossini, Donizetti
5. A schoolmaster
6. Antonio Salieri
7. The Erl-King, Wandering, The Trout...other answers possible
8. Joseph Haydn
9. Michael Vogl
10. 1828

Answers: Schumann

1. Germany
2. "The Happy Farmer," "A March for Little Soldiers," "Sitting by the Fireside,""What they Sing in Church," other answers may be accepted.
3. "The Happy Farmer"
4. Ignaz Moscheles
5. Hawthorne, Longfellow, Whittier, and Lincoln.
6. Longfellow, Hawthorne
7. Frederick Wieck
8. Clara Wieck, daughter of his teacher

9. Was daughter of Schumann's teacher, had eight children, played piano well, composed, lived forty years after husband died.

10. the Leipzig Conservatory

11. Mendelssohn, Chopin, Brahms

12. "This is the way the farmer walks when he comes home singing from his work."

13. Niels Gade

14. 1810

15. music for the piano, songs, and symphonies.

16. He was the head of a musical newspaper, which is still remembered because of the great work he did in helping people to find out new composers.

17. He used a machine that he thought was going to help him play better. It hurt his hand so that he was never able to play well again. In his last years, he went out of his mind,and died insane at the age of 46.

Answers: Verdi

1. Roncole, Italy, October 10, 1813

2. 88

3. a string quartet, The Manzoni Requiem, and a National Hymn.

4. Answers will vary.

5. Organ and spinetta

6. 1839

7. Othello and Falstaff

8. farming

9. A little piano

10. Milan

11. thirty

12. Egypt

13. He founded the Casa di Riposo (House of Rest), a home for aged musicians.

Answers: Wagner

1. operas
2. May 22nd, 1813
3. Liszt, Schumann, Verdi, and Chopin
4. Answers will vary.
5. Die Meistersinger
6. Walter
7. A fussy old schoolmaster kind of a man
8. Hans Sachs
9. He had such a hard time with the ong, he broke down and did not finish it.
10. People like ourselves, as well as gods and goddesses, giants and Rhine maidens, and Nibelungs.
11. Wotan and Donner are gods. Freia is a goddess Fafner is a giant. Mime is a Nibelung.
12. Red and White Lion
13. Read poetry, loved animals, went to classical school, translated twelve books of the Odyssey into German, played the piano, read "Romeo and Juliet" in English, wrote a play.
14. von Weber
15. Der Freischütz
16. that we carry them into adulthood

About the Author

Gail McGaffigan is also the author of several books for young people (and the young-at-heart), including THE ADVENTURES OF LITTLE PANSY, 1862 and THE FAIRY TALE ALPHABET, as well as THE CLASSICAL SPELLER, a spelling curriculum for grades 1 - 8. She lives in coastal New England with her husband and children, and holds a Master's degree from the Boston University College of Fine Arts. Mrs. McGaffigan is currently at work on a companion textbook for her free, one-year music appreciation course, *Classically Gail*, found at the address below.

She may be contacted by the following methods:

Blog: https://www.classicallygail.blogspot.com
E mail: https://www.classicallygail@yahoo.com

Blog: https://www.lovinglyrestored.blogspot.com
E mail: https://www.lovinglyrestored@yahoo.com

*****

Sample Other Books Now by Gail McGaffigan

Enjoy these bonus selections from three of Gail McGaffigan's retro series, *The Julia Carroll Chronicles* and *The Hope Lockhart Mysteries*. and true British crime selections from the files of Inspector Thomas Waters. The first two series are mainly aimed at the Nancy Drew set, and include special sections of authentic recipes and activities from the early 20th century. The last is for mystery lovers ages 12 through adult.

The Mystery of the Blue Mill. 1913

CHAPTER 1 Starting a New Life

The wheels hummed in the ears of Julia Carroll for hours, as she sat on the comfortable seat in the last car of the afternoon Limited, the train whirling her through green valleys, from the West to the East. It had been a very long journey for the girl, but Julia knew that it would soon come to an end. Chartley was not many miles ahead now; she had figured it out, using the railroad's schedule and map. As the stations flew by, she had read their names with her quick eyes, until dusk fell, and she could no longer see more than the signal lamps and switch targets, as the train whirled on.

She stared through the window. This last car of the train was fairly full, but she had been lucky to have a seat all to herself. She was glad, too, because anyone seated next to her might have discovered how hard it was for her to keep back the tears. Julia Carroll had never been a crybaby, and she wasn't about to start now.

"We had all that out weeks ago, you know we did," she whispered to herself, stuffing down that inner part that really wanted to break the bravery pact. "when we learned we had to leave good old Morristown, and Miss True Pettis, and Patsy Michaels, and-- and all our other good friends...."

....."No, Julia Carroll! Uncle Everett Wells may be a very nice man...and to live in a mill...a blue mill! That ought to make up for a whole slew of disappointments-- "

Her thoughts were interrupted by a light tap upon her shoulder. Julia glanced around quickly. She saw, standing beside her, a tall, old gentleman, who had been sitting two seats behind, on the other side of the aisle, ever since the train left Buffalo.

He was a thin, old man, with an eagle-beaked face, and a sweeping iron-gray mustache. His iron-gray hair waved over the collar of his black coat-- a regular mane of hair which flowed out from under the brim of his soft, well-kept hat. His face would have seemed very stern, if it had not been for the little twinkle in his bright, brown eyes.

"Why don't you do it?" he asked Julia, softly.

"Why don't I do what, sir?" she said, with a little gulp, as that dratted lump rose in her throat again.

"Why don't you cry?" questioned the strange, old gentleman, still speaking softly and with that little twinkle in his eye.

"Well, I have made up my mind not to cry, sir." Now, Julia could smile a little, though the corners of her mouth trembled a bit.

The gentleman sat down beside her, even though she had not asked him. She wasn't afraid of him; she even felt a little glad to have some company. "Tell me all about it," he suggested, with such confidence and interest, that Julia felt more comfortable toward this fatherly man.

It was a little hard to begin; but when he told her that he, too, was going home to Chartley, it became easier. "I am Dr. Davidson," he said. "If you are going to live in Chartley, you will hear all about me, and I can tell you,first-hand, all about the place." His eyes twinkled more than ever, though his stern mouth never relaxed.

"I think my new home is a little way outside of Chartley," Julia said, timidly. "They call it the Blue Mill."

The humor faded from his bright expression, but, even then, his face still seemed kind. "Everett Wells' mill," he said, thoughtfully.

"Yes, sir. That is my uncle's name."

"Your uncle?"

"My great uncle, to be exact," said Julia. "He was my mom's uncle."

"Then, you," he said, speaking even more gently than before, "are little Mary Wells' daughter?"

"Mom was Mary Wells before she married Dad," said Julia, more easily now. "She died four years ago."

He nodded, looking away from her, out of the window at the twilight landscape, which hurried by them.

"Poor Dad died last winter. I stayed with friends, after he died," Julia continued, bravely. "They wrote to Uncle Everett and he-- he said I could come and live with him and Aunt Alice Browning."

In a flash the twinkle came back into his eyes, and he nodded again. "Ah, yes! Aunt Allie," he said. "I had forgotten Aunt Allie." He seemed pleased to remember her.

"She keeps house for Uncle Everett, I understand," Julia continued. "But she isn't my aunt."

"She is everybody's Aunt Allie, I think," said Doctor Davidson, with a grin.

For some reason this made Julia feel better. He spoke as though she would love Aunt Allie, and Julia had left so many kind friends behind her in Morristown, that she was glad to hear that somebody in her new home was going would be kind to her.

Miss True Pettis had not shown her Uncle Ev's letter, and Julia was afraid that her uncle (whom she had never even met) was not exactly thrilled about Julia's coming to the Blue Mill. Miss True and most of her Morristown friends had been poor people, so Julia had felt that she could not remain a burden on them.

Somehow, she did not have to explain all this to Doctor Davidson. He seemed to understand it, when he nodded and his eyes twinkled so glowingly. "Chartley is a pleasant town. You will like it," he said, cheerfully. "The Blue Mill is five miles out, on the Lake Owlbright Road. It is pretty country. It will be dark when you ride over it tonight; but you will like it when you see it by daylight." He took it for granted that Uncle Everett would come to the station to meet her, and that comforted Julia a lot.

"You will pass my house on that road," continued Doctor Davidson. "but when you come to town you must not pass it."

"Excuse me?" she asked him, surprised.

"Not without stopping to see me," he explained, his eyes twinkling more than ever. Then, he left her and went back to his seat.

Julia found, when he had gone, that the choke came back into her throat again, and the sting of tears to her eyes...but she would not let those tears fall! She stared out of the window and saw that it was now very dark. The whistle of the fast-flying locomotive shrieked its long warning, and a group of signal lights flashed past. Then, she heard the loud ringing of a gong at a grade crossing. They must be nearing Chartley now.

Then, she knew that they were on a sharp curve, for she saw the lights of the locomotive and the mail car far ahead upon the gleaming rails. They began to slow down, too, and the wheels wailed under the pressure of the brakes. She could see the signal lights along the tracks ahead and then-- with a start, for she knew what it meant-- a sharp blue flame appeared out of the darkness, beyond the rushing engine pilot.

31

Danger! That is what that blue lamp meant. The brakes clamped down upon the wheels again, so suddenly that the easily-riding coach jarred through all its parts. The blue eye winked out instantly, but the long and heavy train came to a sudden stop.

For information on how to purchase a paperback copy: http://www.amazon.com/The-Mystery-Blue-Mill-1913/dp/1479234435/ref=sr_1_15?ie=UTF8&qid=1350079782&sr=8-15&keywords=gail+mcgaffigan https://www.smashwords.com/profile/view/gailmcgaffigan

For information on how to purchase the Kindle Edition: http://www.amazon.com/Mystery-Julia-Carroll-Chronicles-ebook/dp/B0094WFGEU/ref=sr_1_3?ie=UTF8&qid=1350079782&sr=8-3&keywords=gail+mcgaffigan

Hope for a Nobody

Hope's train left early in the morning, and her uncle went to the station with her. Mrs. Andrews cried a great deal when she said good-bye, but Hope cheered her up by describing the long, chatty letters they would write to each other, and by assuring her that she might visit her in California. Mr. Lockhart placed his niece in the care of the conductor and the porter, and the last person Hope saw was this gray-haired uncle running beside the train, waving his hat and smiling at her, till her car passed beyond the platform.

"Now," said Hope methodically, "if I think back, I will cry; so I'll think ahead." This she proceeded to do. She pictured Mrs. Jeter as a gray-haired, capable, kindly woman, older than Mrs. Andrews, and perhaps more calm. She might like to be called "Aunt Anna.'" Mr. Jeter, she decided, would be short and round, with twinkling blue eyes and, perhaps, a white, stubby beard. He would probably call her "Sis," and would always be studying how to make things about the house comfortable for his wife. "I hope they have horses, pigs, cows, and sheep," mused Hope, the flying landscape slipping past her window unheeded. "And if they have sheep, they'll have a dog. Wouldn't I love to have a dog to take long walks with! And, of course, there will be a flower garden. 'Brier Farm' sounds like a bed of roses to me."

The idea of roses persisted, and while Hope, outwardly, was strictly attentive to the things about her, giving up her ticket at the proper time, playing Royal Wedding with her deck of cards, drinking the cocoa, and eating the sandwich the porter brought her at eleven o'clock (on Uncle Richard's orders, she learned); she was, in reality, busy picturing a white farmhouse set in the center of a rose garden, with a hedge of hollyhocks dividing it from a scarcely-less-beautiful and orderly vegetable kingdom.

It was all daydreams, she was soon to learn.

CHAPTER 6: The Nobody

"THE next station's yours, Miss," said the porter, breaking in on Hope's reflections. "Any small luggage? No? All right, I'll see that you get off safely."

Hope gathered up her coat and stuffed the scarcely-read magazine she had bought from the train boy, into her bag. Then, she carefully put on her pretty, grey, silk gloves and tried to see her face in the mirror of her little purse. She wanted to look nice when the Jeters first saw her. The train jarred to a standstill.

Hope hurried down the aisle, to find the porter waiting for her with his little step. She was the only person to leave the train at Hoxie Corners, and, happening to glance down the line of cars, she saw her trunk, the one solitary piece of baggage, tumbled clumsily to the platform. The porter, with his step, swung aboard the train, which began to move slowly out. Hope felt unaccountably small and deserted standing there, and as the platform of the last car swept past her, she was conscious of a lump in her throat.

"Hello!" blurted an oddly attractive voice at her shoulder, a boy's voice, shy and quick but with a sturdy directness that promised strength and honesty. The cornflower-blue eyes into which Hope turned to look were honest, too, and the shock of yellow hair and the half-embarrassed grin that displayed a set of slightly uneven, white teeth instantly put the girl in favor of the speaker. There was a splash of brown freckles across the snub nose, and the tanned cheeks and blue overalls told Hope that a country boy stood before her.

"Hello!" she said politely. "You're from Mr. Jeter's, aren't you? Did they send you to meet me?"

"Yes, Mr. Jeter said I was to fetch you," replied the boy. "I knew it was you, 'cause no one else got off the train. If you'll give me your trunk-check, I'll help the agent put it in the wagon. He locks up and goes home in a little while."

Hope produced the check and the boy disappeared into the little, one-room station. The girl, for the first time, looked around her. Hoxie Corners was not much of a place, judging from the station. The station, itself, was not much more than a shack, sadly in need of paint and without the tiny patch of Goodwin lawn that often makes the plainest railroad station pleasant to the eye. Cinders filled in the road and the ground around the platform. Hitched to a post, Hope now saw a thin sorrel horse, harnessed to a rickety spring wagon, with a board laid across it, in place of a seat. To her astonishment, she saw her trunk lifted into this wagon by the station agent and the boy who had spoken to her.

"Why--why, it doesn't look very comfortable," said Hope to herself. "I wonder if that's the best wagon Mr. Jeter has. Maybe his good horses are busy, or the carriage is broken, or something."

The boy unhitched the sorry nag and drove up to the platform where Hope was waiting. He blushed under his tan as he jumped down to help her in. "I'm afraid it isn't nice enough for you," he said, glancing with admiration at Hope's dress. "I spread that salt bag on the seat, so you wouldn't get rust from the nails in that board on your dress. I'm awfully sorry I don't have a robe to put over your lap."

"Oh, I'm all right," Hope hastened to assure him tactfully. Then, with a desire to put him at his ease, "Where is the town?" she asked. They had turned from the station straight into a country road, and Hope had not seen a single house.

"Hoxie Corners is just a station," explained the boy. "Mostly milk is shipped from it. All the trading is done at Peacedale. There's stores, and schools, and a good-sized town there. Mr. Jeter had you come to Hoxie Corners 'cause it's half a mile nearer than Peacedale. The horse has lost a shoe, and he doesn't want to run up a blacksmith's bill till the foot gets worse than it is."

Hope's brown eyes widened with amazement. "That horse is limping now," she said severely. "Do you mean to tell me Mr. Jeter will let a horse get a sore foot before he'll pay out a little money to have it shod?"

The boy turned and looked at her with something burning in his face that she did not understand. Hope was not used to bitterness. "Bob Jeter," declared the boy stiffly, "would let his own wife go without shoes, if he thought she could get through as much work as she can with 'em. Look at my feet!" He thrust out a pair of rough, heavy work shoes, the toes patched sloppily, the laces knotted in half a dozen places. Hope noticed that the heel of one was ripped, so that the boy's skin showed through. "Let his horse go to save a blacksmith's bill!" repeated the lad angrily. "I should think he would! The only thing in this world that counts with Bob Jeter is money!"

Hope's heart sank. To what kind of a home had she come ? Her head was beginning to ache, and the glare of the sun on the white, dusty road hurt her eyes. She wished that the wagon had some kind of top, or that the board seat had a back. "Is it very much further?" she asked wearily.

"I'll bet you're tired," said the boy quickly. "We still have three miles to go yet. The sorrel can't make very good time, even at his best, but I aim to favor his sore foot, even if I do get cheated out of my dinner,"

"I'm so hungry," declared Hope, restored to life at the thought of food. "All I had on the train was a cup of hot chocolate and a sandwich. Aren't you hungry, too?"

"Considering that all I've had since breakfast at six this morning, is an apple I stole while hunting through the orchard for the turkeys, I'd say I'm starved," admitted the boy. "But I'll have to wait till six to-night, and so will you."

"But I haven't had any lunch!" Hope protested loudly. "Of course, Mrs. Jeter will let me have something-- perhaps they'll wait for me."

The boy pulled on the lines mechanically as the sorrel stumbled. "If that horse goes down once, he'll die in the road, and that'll be the first rest he's known in seven years," he said. "No, Miss, the Jeters won't wait for you. They wouldn't wait for their own

mother, and that's a fact: I remember seeing the old lady, who was senile the year before she died, crying up in her room, because no one had called her to breakfast, and she came down too late to get any. Mrs. Jeter puts dinner on the table at twelve sharp, and whoever's not there has to wait till the next meal. Bob Jeter figures it's that much food saved, and he's got no intention of having late-comers gobble it up."

Hope Lockhart's straight, little chin lifted. She was not one to back down in the face of injustice, and her fighting spirit rose to combat without much encouragement. "My uncle's paying my board, and I intend to eat," she announced firmly. "I guess I'm upsetting the household by coming so late in the afternoon; but there was no other train till night. I have some chocolate and crackers in my bag--suppose we eat those now?"

"Gee, that will be fine!" the fresh voice of the boy beside her was charged with appreciation. "There's a spring up the road a ways, and we'll stop and get a drink. Chocolate sure will taste good."

Hope was quicker to observe than most girls of her age, her grief having taught her to see other people's troubles. As the boy drew rein at the spring and leaped down to bring her a drink from its cool depths, she noticed how thin he was and how red and calloused were his hands.

"Thank you," she smiled, giving back the cup. "That's the coldest water I ever tasted. I'm all cooled off now." He climbed up beside her again, and the wagon creaked on its journey. As Hope divided the chocolate and crackers, quietly giving her driver the larger portion, she asked his name. "I suppose you know I'm Hope Lockhart," she said. "You've probably heard Mrs. Jeter say she went to school with my Uncle Richard. Tell me who you are, and then we'll be introduced."

The mouth of the boy twisted curiously, and a sullen look came into the blue eyes.

"You can do without knowing me," he said shortly. "But as long as you'll hear me yelled at from sun-up to sun-down, I might as well make tell you my claim to greatness: I'm 'that nobody from the poorhouse'--I understand if you want to move over now"

"You have no right to talk like that," Hope said quietly. "I haven't given you any reason to. And if you are really from the poorhouse, you must be an orphan like me. Can't we be friends? Besides, I don't know your name even yet."

The boy looked at the girl's sweet face and his own cleared. "I'm a pig!" he muttered with shame. "My name's Chris Harris, Miss. I hadn't any call to flare up like that...but living with the Jeters doesn't teach a fellow very good manners. I am from the poorhouse. Bob Jeter took me when I was ten years old. I'm thirteen now."

"I'm twelve," said Hope. "Don't call me Miss, it sounds so stiff. I'm Hope. Oh, dear, how dreadfully lame that horse is!" The poor beast was limping, and in evident pain.

Chris explained that there was nothing they could do, except to let him walk slowly and try to keep him on the soft edge of the road. "He'll have to go five miles tomorrow, to get to the blacksmith's in Peacedale," he said moodily. "I'm ashamed to drive a horse through the town in the shape this one's in."

Hope thought indignantly that she would write to the S. P. C. A.. They must have agents throughout the country, she knew, and surely it could not be within the law for any farmer to allow his horse to suffer, as the sorrel was plainly suffering. "Is Mr. Jeter poor, Chris?" she ventured timidly. "I'm sure Uncle Richard thought Brier Farm a fine, large place. He wanted me to learn to ride horseback this summer."

"It'll have to be on a sawhorse," replied Chris ironically. "You bet Jeter isn't poor! Some say he's worth a hundred thousand, if he's worth a penny...but tight-fisted--say, that man's so tight, he puts every penny through the wringer. You've come to a fine place, make no mistake, Hope. I'm kind of sorry to see a girl get caught in the Jeter machine."

"I won't stay, unless I like it," declared Hope quickly. "I'll write to Uncle Richard, and you can come, too, Chris.... Why are we turning in here?"
"This," said Chris Harris pointing with his whip dramatically, "is Brier Farm."

This title coming soon!

The Revenge

<u>1.</u>

1841

Splashed across the morning rags were sensational headlines about the Swiss felon, Levasseur, and his cronies. After sailing for the penal settlements, their convict-ship, the Amphytrim, had been lost in frigid waters off the French coast. The drowning of her crew and prisoners had created quite a stir in England.

I read the account of the tragedy in the newspaper with mixed feelings: relief that Levasseur would not be returning to English soil in two years, after all, but regret for the untimely death of his co-conspirator, Le Breton, whom I regarded as more of a sheep than a scheming wolf.

The paper went into the dustbin, soon to be as forgotten as the day's coffee grounds. Nearly a year of daily life would jostle the shipwreck from my mind, before a terrible fiasco would recall it, and I would receive a grim reminder of how like an ocean storm hate can be, when nurtured in a certain mindset.

A robbery of a precious metal relics (silver chalices and whatnot) had been committed in Portman Square, with clever boldness that left no doubt that it had been a most professional job. Since the first round of detectives had failed to uncover the offenders, the many threads of the case were placed in my hands, to see if my renowned dexterity (or "luck," as my fellow officers referred to it) would help me solve the crime.

Witnesses' implicated a local ne'er-do-well named Martin (when he wasn't going by one of his many aliases), who had been lurking nearby the burgled house prior to the crime. A reward of fifty pounds was offered for his capture and conviction.

I conducted the investigation with my usual energy and vigilance, without turning up a single new fact. I did not discover any clue to the missing property in the pawn shops or classified ads. The artifacts had successfully eluded all chances of recovery.

The only hope was that an increased reward might get one of the gang to betray his confederates. The stolen goods were of great value, so this was done: one hundred guineas was offered for information leading to the recovery of the stolen articles.

I went to the printer's shop to order the posters announcing the increased reward. After enjoying a long gossip with my old friend, Jencks, the printer, I was walking through Ryder's Court, Newport Market, at about a 10:15 PM, when a tall man passed me swiftly, holding a scarf to his face. There was nothing odd in that, as the weather was bitterly cold and sleety, so I walked on, thinking nothing of it.

I was just leaving the court, moving towards Leicester Square, when swift steps sounded behind me. I instinctively turned; and as I did so, a vicious stab grazed my left shoulder, aimed, no doubt, at the back of my neck. It was the same tall person who had passed me a minute before! He ran off like a deer, the muffler still clutched to his face. The blow, sudden, jarring, and inflicted with a sharp instrument — a stout knife or dagger — sent my head reeling. By the time I recovered from it, all chance of successful pursuit had passed. I had the injury, a mere flesh wound, dressed at the chemist's shop in the Haymarket.

Since reporting the attack would gain nothing towards capturing the perpetrator, I said little about it to anyone. I managed to conceal it entirely from my wife, the lovely and ever-patient Alice, who certainly did not need further cause for worry whenever I was detained at work.

It frustrated me no end to think that I had come that close to the criminal, without a clue as to his identity. To be sure, he ran at an amazing and unusual pace, but nimble feet were a quality possessed by so many of the light-fingered clients encountered in my professional life, that it did little to narrow the field of suspects to a workable number. I decided to forget the unpleasant incident as soon as possible.

This title coming soon!

Printed in Great Britain
by Amazon.co.uk, Ltd.,
Marston Gate.